NEWS FROM INSIDE
A Poetry Anthology

Edited by Estrellita Mendez

Hand Maid Books

in association with

Bombshelter Press
Los Angeles

News From Inside
A Poetry Anthology
Edited by Estrellita Mendez

Cover Photographs by Sunni Donmoyer

News From Inside

ISBN 0-941017-35-4

Manufactured in the United States of America

Hand Maid Books

in association with

Bombshelter Press
6421-1/2 Orange Street
Los Angeles, California 90048

For Nick

TABLE OF CONTENTS

(i)

James Baldwin
from
"The Creative Process"
The Price of the Ticket, Collected Nonfiction 1948-1985

"Perhaps the primary distinction of the artist is that he must actively cultivate that state which most men, necessarily, must avoid: the state of being alone. . . . Most of us are not compelled to linger with the knowledge of our aloneness, for it is a knowledge that can paralyze all action in this world. . . . But the conquest of the physical world is not man's only duty. He is also enjoined to conquer the great wilderness of himself. The precise role of the artist, then, is to illuminate that darkness, blaze roads through that vast forest, so that we will not, in all our doing, lose sight of its purpose, which is, after all, to make the world a more human dwelling place."

● ● ● ● ● ● ● ● ●

William Carlos Williams
from
William Carlos Williams and James Laughlin, Selected Letters

"You know I've been thinking a lot recently about the old dreamers. . . . It's the dream all right but it's to be lost in the dream, to be so taken up by what I term the reality of the dream that appears to me to offer the greatest satisfaction I can imagine.

". . . I came across a statement by Lionel Trilling . . . He said the more our lives are chemically determined by our environment to despair and destruction, the greater the need for the poem. . . . It . . . taught me that between pessimism and despair there is a tremendous chasm. Despair, yes, but not pessimism and the difference is the dream. *That* they cannot hold by a halter and that, by God, is the real."

The poets represented in these pages come from diverse backgrounds, yet, like everyone else, they share the basic challenge of balancing career, family and duty to others with the struggle to achieve some measure of personal fulfillment. What distinguishes them is their willingness, their need, to heed the call of the muse within. To undertake the responsibilities that come with accepting the mantle of "poet."

No one who has ever sat down before the blank page would claim that making poems is easy work. It's tricky business to step into that great wilderness called the self and emerge with some discovery, some truth to be carried forward and made known. What makes the journey worthwhile is the dreamlike state of creation -- the falling into the "reality of the dream" -- where the artifice of the day-to-day is stripped away. This dream state is neither a sleep nor a forgetting. The knowledge that is garnered in that state, the special texture of individual experience made universal, is what poetry reveals.

It is not a casual inclination to make oneself the subject of scrutiny, yet poets do that. If Williams is right when he says that, "it is difficult to get the news from poems," then it may also be true that people "die miserably every day for lack of what is found there." These poets have attempted to save their own lives in making their poems. Now they come to share, to bring you the news that you can't get from the "news." Mined from the great estates of themselves, they offer up their news -- from inside.

Read all about it.

Estrellita Mendez

NEWS FROM INSIDE

Mimi's Finger

That finger
still crooked
clasping a sterile sheet,
puffed blueberry splotch
where the I.V. tech slipped.
That finger
connected to a small body
missing a few parts:
Thyroid, cataracts, breast tissue and muscle
surgically strip mined
scraped down to the rib cage
Harvested from a young farmer's wife
with no health insurance
no voice to protest . . .
Eggs, tubes, a dropped uterus
that exploded like a fallen overripe pear
carrying an eighth child.

An index finger
crooked at the joint closest the tip
Housemaid's finger
made for digging in corners
ready to search a small ear
packed with enough dirt to plant potatoes
That finger
perfectly configured to flute the crust
of a homemade pie
One hand slowly turning the dish
That finger -- cocked -- thwacking the dough
That bent finger
lovingly parting a section of long hair to braid
That finger in cahoots with a thumb
to pinch a grandchild's cheek
or plumpish biscuits.

6

That finger
tapping a tabletop
at the Knights of Columbus
ready to push a plastic chit in place
and yell -- Bingo!
That finger
gripping the top
of a carefully rinsed orange juice can
doubling as a dice tossing Yahtzee cup

That finger
making the sign of the cross
silently seeking salvation
clean
always about coming clean
dipping into holy water, bath water, well water,
dish water, scrub water
always about coming clean

When I poke into corners of my young son's ears
I sometimes look for signs of that finger
I imagine how she'd
cradle his head
when my back was
turned how she'd check
those tiny ears for pay dirt.
My son
the only promise she ever broke to me.
A promise I needed to believe
so I wouldn't cry too hard
the last time I saw her finger,
crooked
clasping that sterile sheet.

To whom this concerns:

I am writing in response to your advertisement
in the Sunday Times.
I need an easy job I am tired. I realize this letter
  I cannot finish this letter this Sunday I will masturbate
soon I'll need beer, grateful to hear from you
but the impermanence of part time work
As my resume indicates I lost the book I bought last week

  The semester is almost over.
My husband is a trumpet sucking in the air
  the obstinacies of children and their terrors and angers
I live with the shakes running every morning sleep with the
beers and the fleas on the floor
with the moon shrinking and thin mattress inchoate
unformed and ugly by the dog mind dust and dog hair the
end of the week I am sick like the party to celebrate the
writing lab I supervise I come in and Laura says when I
take off my shades you look sad!

I cried driving in hearing the good radio music because I
lost my job I cried on the way in you all looking at me
I got out of the car I parked and looked about.
You are all me I said seeing this seeing that you are me
planted cypress stiff green and stub, limbed heads lobbed
off by groundskeepers
you are me I laughed at the vast wan cement building ahead
I said to the pigeon red feet and puffed up grey
iridescent neck you are me   spear of bird song
the chain link fence the soft wind passes through
And each time I was right
the telephone poles 3 rows of four
set up for the students to climb to prepare
for a career in cable TV repair
they are aloof and stripped

tall and cut off and everywhere flat tar
absorbs oil drips, you are me the limp tension of
telephone wires quiet and slack,
   the big broad spread of the
tree, arms to the sky,
the random scatter of brown yellow leaves and needles and
twigs and the ant, you are me, tiny diligence,
the blur of asphalt flecks and glints as I go
upstairs and down corridors, the door,
I was right each time you are me to the
brown door, a quick bird in the grass
then I am in the lab, and I remember the particles of dust
in the kitchen that waft and suck into the vortex of a
person leaving.

A Man's Attention

I go to Beef Bowl for lunch
'cause all I have is
a pocketful of change.
I sit near the front window
and watch the women
walking by.
There are tall ones,
short ones,
thin ones
and fat ones.
Some have pants on,
others wear dresses.
I like the ones who wear dresses, best.
I like to see a woman's legs,
the curve of her calves,
the twists of her muscles
as they dance
on heels too high,
too limiting
for anything
but catching
a man's attention . . .
to catch my attention.
I am a man.

Regret

Regret is a 12 x 14 charcoal of your ex-wife,
wrapped in a blanket,
laying in your leaky car trunk
that's seen so many rains
the face has bled from the canvas
and there's only traces,
vague memories you hold in your heart,
you are reminded of when it rains salty tears
down your lined cheeks,
burning your flesh
with thoughts of
your better half,
wrapped in a blanket,
laying in a trunk,
bleeding.

Try Not

Try not to owe something,
anything
to somebody.
Try not owing the next call
the next lunch
the next cue
to become slow
and therapeutic-like.
Try that.
Try not owing the smile
and the next comment that is meant to appease
everything else that was just said.

My Dream

In my dream last night
I assisted a weak but powerful, corpulent,
slime bucket pasty-assed film industry executive.
Which tasks I performed for him I cannot say.
It seems I was around to assist in his happiness.
I did that with a certain slowness of movement and
relaxed smile.
I flexed my considerable muscles unobtrusively
which contrasted dramatically to his flaccid, floppy,
wasted, white skin.
Instead of making him feel physically inferior to me
it strengthened him because he felt safer with my body
than he did with his. In my presence his movements
became more fluid. His gestures followed a longer arc.
He was happier with me around.
I don't know what he was paying me.
Money wasn't the reason I was there.
My attitude was one of benevolence.
I was assisting a larger design that I could not know.
Time was not a factor.
There was no duration to my servitude.
I embraced my pleasure when I could.
I was courting a young girl of sweet skin and copper eyes.
She had not yet been touched and
it was my desire to loosen her covering
with my patient hands.
We both wanted to hear our hearts race,
to feel our breath shorten,
our apertures enlarge.
Our joint understanding occurred from a distance.
We were moving closer to one another.
My assisting the pig and courting the girl was the
turning wheel of my existence and
neither would happen without the other.

Sweeney

I can't believe that I was crying when I don't even know why. I have been crying inside for months wishing I could break loose from the fears that keep me locked in my cage all alone. My parents gave me a yellow parakeet for my twenty-first birthday. I loved that bird but could never get him to sing for me. Sweeney sang when I wasn't in the room, and my neighbors complained about Sweeney's singing, but I never heard him. One April morning I opened my front door and squinted at the sun as I carried Sweeney's gold cage downstairs, placed it on the grass and then sat with my legs crossed next to the cage. I slid the cage door open. Sweeney wouldn't budge. He just sat in the cage. "Sing, Sweeney," I said. I lowered my head so that I could see his eyes, and when he looked at me he seemed confused and scared. I began to cry and said "Be free, Sweeney." I put his food outside the cage but still, he would not move. Sweeney would not sing for me. It hurt me that Sweeney wouldn't fly away. So, I picked up the cage that seemed so heavy, walked upstairs, brought the cage inside and placed it on the kitchen table. Then I poured myself a cup of coffee and sat down to read the paper.

Going Home

I'm sitting at the desk in my old bedroom
and the door is open a crack, so that
I can see down the hall. It's hard
to believe that this is the same
house I grew up in, because the
walls are a gallery for ancient
family photographs and there are
none of my drawings or posters anymore.

The trundle bed that I loved as a
child has been replaced by a twin bed
with a $600 custom-made ecru bedspread.

In the past eight years, my parents
have decorated the house two, maybe three
times. Thank God it's on the same street,
or else I might not recognize it.

I have no memories of my childhood.
The stories I tell friends are seen through
the eyes of my father and mother or other
relatives who have repeated them to me
time and time again.

My first clear memory is leaving for college
when the bedrooms were being torn up so that
we had to walk on wood planks to get to the garage.
All the images before that are a blur, running
together so that it's difficult to tell where
one
ends
and the
next
begins.

Once

In the beginning is the dark
that place in me where I
find myself
in the darkness at the beginning
of an explosion before the light
obliterates the safe places
obliterates the rest
In the beginning is the agony of light
on eyes unaccustomed to anything
other than an inward look
this light radiating outward with
ferocity, racing towards the edge
of day, fighting to keep back
the inevitable
this beginning that contains the seed
of its own end
the light that runs out at the edge
of a galaxy
leaving me only the feeling of the dark
the enveloping night full of not-day,
of not-light, of not this place I have come
to call my life
In the beginning is a hand in the dark
groping for flesh under a blanket
In the beginning is a tongue run rough
against the pores on my neck
In the beginning is the crack of a collarbone
as the child falls off a chair
In the beginning is the surgeon's knife
splitting flesh to reach an appendix
next to my small heart

In the beginning is tea on the sand
at sunset on a Laguna beach
In the beginning is a woman telling her sister
goodbye at a Dublin train station and not saying
anything to the land she will not see again
In the beginning is a lie
In the beginning is nothing
It is dark
there are no stars
there is no sun
In the beginning is an idea divorced from its
womb
There is never a beginning
only this continuing stretch of black ink
looking for the rest of the gene pool
that lets dinosaurs die
and fleas jump 17 times their length
In the beginning is my hand on his
In the end, it is my hand in my own

Hunger

A man casts his net
into the sea in hunger
and pulls back
nothing but plankton and weed.
He casts the empty net
over and over again.
Eventually, his hunger is gone,
he puts his net back by the dunes
and sits on a bench,
watching the crowds all day
and the movement of the moon at night.
He starts to think
of his dead children
and the way it used to be,
notices the weekend tourists,
and thinks that time,
like an old clock,
moves differently now.

As the elements etch deep lines
in his face, he feels himself
yearn for the next day with passion,
no longer as an enemy or a threat,
and every morning at dawn
he stares through
the dull growing light in the sky,
the only hunger he will now satisfy.

18

South Bend In February

I don't know my father
as he gives me directions
from his Mother's house
to the cemetery where
my Mother lies waiting.
Not finding her,
he goes in to get directions
and I stare at the dashboard
of the rented car,
listening to Bach.
He returns breathless and pale
with a map to dead bodies,
an 'X' where Mom should be.
The trees are bare,
their leaves long since
dropped, raked in and burned --
the dead foliage
a brief, sweet scent
in the Midwestern autumn air.
Below the grey sky,
we stand staring
at the tombstone.
He should pay someone
to clean the site he says,
as I kick dirt, twigs off the stone.

Frog Legs

Joey is licking my foot
how wonderful it feels,
warm and soft.

I'm looking out into the backyard
not my usual view.
When I sit on the other end
of our circular couch
the end next to the telephone
and the basket of meditation books.

I look out and see
the clear blue water of the pool
the purple and pink flowers of verbena
the bushes of yellow and green.
It's beautiful
and as I take it in,
in a full breath
I feel content.
I watch as the pool sweep
ambles around the bottom of the pool
and I think of a child swimming.

I was on a hunt.
My job was to catch the frog
before he did some unthinkable thing.
And I never did know
what my Dad's fear was.
But there I was,
nine years old
diving into cold water
and doing my job
as quickly as my arms
and legs could take me.

I remember having some interesting jobs.
Probably the most peculiar was
to check the toilet for rats.
It was at the Trailer Park we owned.

We would go up every weekend.
The house was vacant during the week
except for things like rats, maybe,
that would try taking a drink of water
from the toilet bowl
and the unlucky ones fell in and drowned.

I suppose I got those odd jobs
because I protested the least.
I was always the most rugged of the lot.
And my Dad,
well he always believed in being the boss,
never did the dirty work.
He would stand around giving orders.
He was good at it.
He liked it.

The times I remember him
in the best of moods
were when we were working together.
He was a handsome man when he smiled
his big blue eyes could sparkle so
and his long thick eyelashes
added to the dazzle.

It was nice to be with my Dad
when he was in a good mood
just to look at him.

My Being In This Place

Smoothed by the flowing
tension of water and sand
it was one in a million
the night the moon flung
silver on the floor.
I painted the sun
on the ceiling
burning my eyes, but
I can see better with them closed.
I can feel the firmness of
a presence, that has become
potent with my being in this place
and its existence will continue
like mine.
We are penetrating preachers.
I revere the tribesmen's
great solidarity.
We are rooted in infinity,
we do not lose ourselves
in the struggle with all the
forces, for one thing only
the glass is only half full
of letters for my poems.
My cat got my tongue
before I can lick the steam
off the window.
The cold wind slices the clouds
into small pieces
that dance a huge circle
around the moon.
Don't be afraid,
look at the earth's winter, naked
as it shivers a lullaby
and waits for the sun.

Wind Gardener

The wind blows.
It rattles and shakes,
pushes, and bends
brussels sprouts
the trees
and my house.
Bones creak and
shadows the wall
to shape the tune.
The willow wails.
Pop corn, the snake sizzles,
grasping at the shadow wind.
It is only the beginning.
Beginning of the storm.
Beginning of the rain.
Rain beginning of the truth.
Truth begins water morning of rain surging,
water flowing to snow to earth.
The road is washed away.
Way down.
Down lower than the hills,
lower than the mountain
drip, mountains daring to rush.
Rushed away and taken.
Take it.
Take the flat lands.
Daring to rush the silence.
Rushed silence,
rivet the rivers.
Drips rushing and shaking,
my hollyhock world.
My eyes are dry
and I am not afraid
to gather up the wind.

Aprons

The young woman on the corner, selling las fruitas,
wears an apron,
blue, with little pockets
where she hides her hands and jingles change,
a white ruffle of trim against the legs
and up in back to wrap her slender thighs.
The fruit sits in new cardboard boxes at the curb.
A bent old lady, waiting for the bus,
points at the apron, they laugh.
I wish there were more reason than a red light
to be here. I would ask her
to peel oranges, bananas,
make me a mixed bowl of fruit,
pour milk with a smile,
a hug and kiss with a spoon.
I would look up then,
from where I was sitting in my little chair,
grateful for this blue apron of sky
the ruffle of clouds just above my head.

Traffic Light

It's still hot even with the windows rolled down,
waiting at the red light on this street,
where the fence around the lumber yard
is topped with 3 strands of barbed wire
on outward leaning supports,
and 3 strands leaning in.
Around them there are corkscrews
of knife-edged razor wire,
stainless and bright.
The barbed wire is rusty.
Deep cuts and tetanus, I think,
make sure anyone climbing this gets it all.
It looks so menacingly defensive.
I feel if I get too close it will reach out and bite me,
like a protective doberman.
It makes me defensive in myself;
this is the kind of stuff
that wraps around souls,
keeping everyone out,
keeping myself in.

So here I am caught in this uncomfortable thought,
when a sparrow pops out of nowhere,
the way little birds do,
landing on a top strand between the barbs
and the rolls of razor,
bouncy, looking around while chirping questions, attitudes,
street-wise statements of a city bird,
and then flitting away as the light goes green,
leaving me and the barbed wire
completely wrapped in its song.

If I Could Cry

The stripes of my bathrobe zoom away from me,
always leaving: I turn my back to them
and stretch belly down.
The hummingbird was somewhere else today;
I saw him yesterday evening when the
sky turned unreal, before dusk.
That time that it always is, the sky
like cream, and never stops.
You can't see the bottom;
it holds the evening in its hand.
If I could cry
I would.

My Single Corner

Fill my bowl with fog and violets,
and reach down that trumpet from yonder;
the horse's flaming tail trails stars
into the lake I dream of,
while the inch-by-inch flatness of the wall
makes my single corner.

Secrets In A Language

Sometimes I see a young brother and sister
talking in the intimate way of children,
barely above a whisper,
sharing secrets in a language I used to know,
and I think of me and Nick when we were nine,
walking down the hill every Saturday
to the Baker Theater, with a dollar each.
50¢ for admission and popcorn for a quarter,
left a quarter more for candy or soda.

We counted off rows of seats
marching down the aisle
to the 26th row of the center section.
That first seat had a flaw
in the leather cushion,
an oval patch where the skin
had been stretched wrong somehow.
We found our way there
even in darkness
when the big theater opened up
to swallow us in its red mouth.
I would reach out my hand for the seat
to read its nubbly birthmark
like an invitation in braille.

I was always sorry for Wile E. Coyote.
Like the Trix Rabbit,
he suffered for his desire,
paid for wanting
and never knew satisfaction,
unless there was some pleasure
in the daily schemes,
the grand gesture
played out against futility.

And somewhere an anvil has just fallen.

In my hands a box of pink and white
candy coated licorice.
The shoop shoop of the train in that box
The little engine that could in that box
I think I can, I think I can.

Desire and possibility
flattened under the anvil.

Kids crunching up the sweetness of
Good & Plenty.

The gummy licorice already planting decay.

The House On The Hill

My friend's mother had died,
And I was coming back from the funeral.
As I drove along Coldwater Canyon, I looked up
And there -- suspended in air
Held up by a few steel poles
Slashed diagonally into concrete slabs
Set into the hill,
Was the house Marshal and Laurie and I lived in
In the happiest years of our lives together.

I looked up at my house
And I saw that the new owners
Had placed high shrubs on the deck
In front of the floor-to-ceiling doors,
Shrubs that blocked out the view . . .
The majestic view of the Santa Monica mountains.

And I remembered how we lay in bed
Looking out at those mountains . . .
I remembered how we lived.
I could see myself
Sitting up in that low bed
That had no headboard
Leaning against the wall
Feet extended out to those mountains.
And I remembered how happy we were --
And I felt young again.

I would look out at those mountains
Covered with green
And layered all the way west to the ocean
And I felt peaceful.

Laurie and I would drive up the mountain
To our little cliff house
Suspended over the hill
She in her car seat -- Me at the wheel --
Swinging hands as we sang
"Home again, home again, jiggety-jig."

I had a premonition back then
That if we ever left that house,
Our happiness would end.
That house was magical to all of us --
To Marshal and to Laurie and to me
And to Lola, our salt and pepper schnauzer.
Our hearts cried when we left
And our lives and our love
Were never the same.

Brush Stroke

I think of all the colors.
Maybe I'm the one who sees the blue
with a dust of clouds. And hears the airplane
as music.
Feels birds sweep around
over me like a dance. Smells the warmth
in the breeze that comes by occasionally.
Loves the grass needing water
up to the cracked, winding asphalt.

At the end of the asphalt the slope leading into
open concrete. And past stairs, behind the glass,
tucked around corners -- there are
the colors I want to hold.
Squeeze out between my fingers to stick
to my hands. White made up of yellow and pink
and light blue. More beautiful than a water lily
I could grow. Leaves of
blue and water green.

Yellow made of grey and white, so warm. So
warm in the winter I'm looking east. Peaches
of green and red and brown. They taste
so much better than the yellow ones I can buy.

I see people moving without
a step and boats skimming on paint. And
as much as I love the faded trees
and worn sky, the flat life is the best.

Property Lines

Next to me are books, phone books,
phone numbers, lines,
links to a world I
ride like a fence.

Just high enough to jump off of
when I feel like dancing and get back on by myself
if someone comes.

Or I can jump down
on the other side
if I need to. Sometimes

I lean out sideways holding
on like a bullrider, but
the fence doesn't move.

I could grab someone's hat if they came by
close.

And I make everyone else use the gate.

33

Voyage

Now on the table
all my friends in ties
waving goodbye.
This voyage.
And so much time
taken to learn again
what we once knew
from each other
and forgot.
It's still daylight
but I can see the moon.
Almost
or so it seems
transparent.
Not even a full moon.
But a full moon.

Butcher

Butcher sipping tea.
Butcher fishing with the cord tied round his neck
    as he leans over the bank, thinking:
    trout or shark.

Butcher notices his mother's getting old.
    Cradles her wrinkled arm in his hand.
    Takes a peek at the other arm in the
    bottom drawer beside the bed.

Butcher's asleep now, so don't disturb him.
    Tip-toe through this part, passing
    his feet sticking out from under the sheets.
    Stop! He's turning over.
    The mountain rearranges itself and crawls
    back into the dream, that deep mouth.

It's morning, he's off to work. His hands clean
    as a baby's.

Butcher's in the bank. His desk neat: each pad,
    pencil, loan request arranged geometrically
    like a Mondrian. Here come the customers!

Butcher checks the vault. Smells new money.

Butcher's at his desk. His foot held above the button
    on the floor. Sips his tea. Waits breathlessly
    for the gun-wielding, stocking-faced, blood-thirsty
    robber.

When The Weekends

When the weekends aren't really weekends
and the not-doing of things
that should be done
builds the guilt wall under the necks of us,
I would reach past the
blood rain and the hair
and take myself out of everything
that is ours
just for this time, anyway,
and I would tear a piece off this tree,
at the soft branch end where it's just a leaf,
and spin it between my fingers
and worry
that this
is what we miss.

I Dwell Too Often

I dwell too often
on tangible tokens
that these feelings aren't my father
and that a rose wrapped
in plastic -- or some such other touch -- somehow
makes it certain, and somehow
proves the pulpit proverb
long burned and done with. Though
then, like pupils, you and I
turn a page to play it out again --
as if, in all our fearing, we can't
bear to forget.
And yet,
we must forget
our fathers, with
their frowning,
and their fumbling,
if only because they too
have fathers
to forget,
and always
to forgive.

Shore Lover

I see a tide pool where a sea anemone attaches
itself to smooth rocks. Tentacles flex without
ceasing, open and close, draw nourishment
from the water, expel it out again.
The water, cold and briny, carries
sand in its tidal flow, setting it down
gently, filling the mouth of the delicate
creature, letting it sift among the
knob-ended fronds, separating the
slender, grasping arms that seem like
waving petals of a marine flower.

I see a man kneel, watching.
He reaches down and, brushing
the sand aside, places his finger
in the polyp's mouth, feeling
the give and gentle sting
of its tentacles. He draws
his finger in and out, revolving
it inside the opening.
Push. Circle. Pull. Remove.
He puts his finger in his mouth and
sucks, tasting the brine, feeling
the particles of sand, grainy in
his mouth, ground by his tongue
against his teeth.
He puts his whole hand into the
pool, stirs it, mixing sand and water,
withdraws his hand and walks away.

The anemone closes its tentacles,
closes in upon itself,
closes against the loss.

Official Decision

Four legs stretch out. Hooves thud into the turf,
then bend back and up, gather, stretch again,
out and up and back. Muscles bunch beneath
the skin, tighten, punch the body through the air.
The wind rushes, parts his mane,
layers it, thick and wet, over his neck, under
slapping reins held by his light rider.
The horse's leg straightens down, below the earth,
into an unseen hole. His body snaps forward with
a crunching sound and he lies convulsing,
his rider, helmet blasted off, sprawls. Still. Limp.

Booten men cross the track to stand and gape.
The horse's bone shoves a white shard through
his skin. The men shake their heads from side to side.

Paramedics come to where the rider lies,
"His back is broken."
"Maybe."
"His neck, too."
"Maybe."
"There's a trickle of blood."
"A little."
"We'll strap him up so he can't move,
fill him full of medications, he won't feel a thing,
won't say a thing. We'll save him for the docs
so they can have a go to see what they can do.
A miracle can happen, you just never know,
and if there is no miracle, well,
that's not our concern."

The horse is lying still. His pain is gone.
The vet, a true humanitarian, used
just one bullet, clean and quick.

39

Days Go By

Days go by and I remember I haven't slept.
Now I'm only half here, too tired to see
what I'm writing. Now I'm ready to be pulled down,
by gravity, into oblivion. But this water
is sweet, so cold it could only be of this world.
It's woman's work keeps me up nights,
making the marriage, making the baby.
Either that, or the water I drink by the quart
pressing hourly to its exit. When I get up
to pee and lie down again, fully awake,
alone with the heat and the sound of the fan,
alone with my marriage and my baby,
I can hear Cleo's light snore, more like a sigh
than a snore, and Jack's deeper one
when he finally lets go. And when he does
he forgets about me. He's alone
the way we're meant to be but only half of us
know it. And what he finds there
has nothing to do with me, so tired and anxious
I could only be of this world.
All his books are there, and his shoes,
and the pipes he collects but doesn't smoke.
But I have to wait here. Awake or asleep,
it makes no difference. I'm somewhere
he's not and have to wait here till morning.

Mark

My face is like my brother's this afternoon:
thin-lipped, though his are thinner;
nostrils pinched like the nostrils you read about
in English novels. My hair is permed and eyebrows
contoured but you can't hide the length of your face
or the proportion of nose and eyes to cheeks and chin.

This morning I thought about him and couldn't stand it
so I went to the zoo. Though I missed the fish,
I felt all live things belonging there.
I expected to stare at the lions
the longest, the wolves and the less-wild
snow leopards, but the apes held my attention,
their prehensile intelligence, sibling eyes
dulled by a boredom I took for regret.
Only the chimpanzees' swollen bright bottoms
advertised love, evolution, forgiveness.

Coming home I got lost until I found the street
I knew and followed it, first in the wrong
direction, then in the right one.
I used to call my brother when I had to take
a new freeway and he would tell me which offramp
to take and which streets undergoing construction
to avoid, and being lost brought me to him
because the body can't forget, instinct
won't let you forget what you owe others
for your safety.
I was safe because I was finally lost,
I couldn't put it off any longer.
Any radio psychologist can tell you that --
the fear is worse than the losing.

Notes From My Mind

My cousins Lollie and Walter,
my friend Bonnie, and I
play mummies,
walk stiff as if wrapped in sheets.
A form of tag.
I am maybe eight or nine.
We are visiting at Bonnie's house in Phoenix
in the forties.
I step behind a door in the kitchen.
I think it is a closet or pantry;
peeking out a crack,
I back up, fall down a flight of stairs,
passing Bonnie's Grandma on the way down.
She screams.
Uncle Irving comes running, carries me upstairs.
I am crying, hit my nose on the cement cellar.
Uncle Irving treats my nose
by pressing the bump
with a silver fifty cent piece.
I get to keep the coin
and the deviated septum
for life.

Splash It On

If God is a perfume bottle
filled with an elixir of beliefs,
splash it on,
drink it in,
spray it on,
like a rain dance.
Shake it up,
pour it out,
Oh White Lily of the Valley,
Downdrain.
Counterclockwise.
Stick the pin in voodoo fetishes. Poison,
sink in slime, Sweet Peas and Morning Glory,
copulate with the cave man.
Sphinx, Desert Rose, beastblood dies.
And time is the lie
that swallows smelling the stench.

She Broke The Rules

I'm walking down Eisenhower --
the only street in Tehran
named after an American idiot
instead of an Islamic idiot --
for all the world like a free man.
The men are busy picking their noses,
scratching their crotches
and exposing pathetic equipment.

The women see nothing, hear nothing, say nothing.
The more nothing they see,
the more the men go insane.
They call every woman a whore,
with the single exception of mother.
Not a one of them has figured out
that this makes each man's mother
every other man's whore.

Instead they talk dirty and wag their weenies,
cop feels and imprison their sisters.

So, when I hear the crowd gasp
I turn just in time to see this lady
swing her purse at arm's length.
The purse is loaded with
powdered brick and plumber's lead.
She hits this guy along side the head
and lays him out, flat on the asphalt.

"Hal-a-fucking-lew-ya," I think.
I don't know what this asshole did,
I just know that he deserved it.

The next thing that crosses my mind
is a picture of this mob of angry morons
beating a single woman to death --
a taste of Islamic justice.

"No goddamn way," I think
puffing out my chest like John Wayne,
flexing righteous biceps,
flashing the heroic glare.
If they want to hassle this
Iranian Joan of Arc, they are going
to have to go through me.

But the men don't do a thing.

About thirty women jump the lady
and right there in the middle
of Eisenhower street
they beat the liberation
clean out of her.

How To Read A Poem

You take it
all of it
in your hands
hold it close against
your waiting
belly
finger stroke
the page
then
lick it
open
make it want to
press its words
close to you
then
kiss each one
with your eyelashes
and swallow it
all of it
into sleep

Speaking With My Other Mouth

I tug at the beard of my other mouth
as the canal out back floods and ebbs
and the carriage rumbles past again
filled
with whispers riding on top.

My beard tugs me back and
I wouldn't mind but
some thing stirs
deep inside
then ebbs and flows
the whispers creaking along
rumbling somewhere
wanting to form the ohs
the perfect ohs
that come
from being nudged
like tapping the box at breakfast
and watching
the ohs fall out and tumble
over each other.

These ohs formed with
the perfect/imperfect roundness
of the lips lined with fur
and the tongue
that isn't there
yet is somewhere
there.

Girl Scouts

The real warning came early,
when I was butted in the head
by a girl called Sheila.
She said I was different,
had frizzy hair that wasn't in
pigtails,
a pot belly that stuck out.
We were eight when we met
at a swimming club for Jewish people.
We weren't as Jewish as her family was.
Her mother emigrated from Poland
before the war and Hitler got to them,
the others in her family.

Sheila was muscular, big calves,
flat stomach, short neck.
Big brown eyes
hair frizzier than mine.
She got the girls in school
to call me names
or else to ignore me,
especially during games.
Kickball, tetherball, lunch.

One day we all carpooled for Girl Scouts.
Six girls, one mother driving.
Five of them jumped on me
to pull my uniform off
in the back seat of the car.
The mother only shifted her hands
on the wheel.

They climbed all over me.
Stubby, nail-bitten hands
grabbing to punch, unsnap snaps
on the green uniform,
rip at the white slip.
They still smelled like Fritos
and milk from lunch.
It wasn't Sheila's mother driving.
Sheila was the leader.
I was quiet,
never made a sound.

My mother wants me
to move back to my hometown,
to the house next door to Sheila's father
and new wife.
I just keep waiting,
thinking it will all blow over.
Like it did before.
A million years ago.

Vapor Locked

On the corner of 7th and B,
I roll my windows down and wait.
Across the street is a house
I wish my grandma lived in.

Grey painted clapboard,
a big front veranda
framed by white pillars,
a porch swing made for talk

and lovers after dark.
That dappled cat patrols
the rose garden.
Next to the hitching post

stand two ancient elms.
I check the topmost branches
where the sun makes
patterns through the leaves

like looking up through water.
Body relaxed, limbs weightless,
I float in cool green.
Water reed hair fans

out from my scalp.
Slow bubbles
rise to the surface.
I must draw air in soon.

Zig Zag

the zig zag line zigs up
dozens of dinosaurs died for my sins
jumped off cliffs

sank into the tar
gladly the stegosaurus
took the meteor in the chest

that I might fill my tank
with Chevron unleaded extra light
pray for Mary at the bar

writing on ground up trees
with her lucky ball point pen
torts for tarts and pterodactyls

precincts of precedents
Jacoby versus Meyers
the sales girl in the black leather skirt

searches for dinosaur bones
on aisle 5 between the garden hoses
zig zag   zig zag

Rituals

I must have read this someplace,
Or maybe someone told me,
But radishes will grow
Before a man can starve to death.
Imagine . . . nothing to eat for days,
Then looking at a solitary radish,
Red, that root.
It might be divided in half,
Then placed on the tongue.
Just think of the cool heat of it . . .

I remember myriad rituals
For survival,
Like the ceremony of making money.
And it's true that I've lived
In a house of discontent.
I've seen the arc of a shooting star.
I know just how cold the moon is.

I've witnessed the complexity
Of melting commitments.
Also, the mystical communion
Of ultimate realities.
It's all a dull ache
Spreading across my shoulders.

My stomach is full of rocks.
There is the sand of five wars in me.
I am up to my armpits in swamp water.
Today is my fifty-third birthday.
I say these things so that you will know:
Do not put your faith in me.
I have not gathered a single seed
with which to plant radishes.

One Night In The Life Of A Poet

All night I conjure up
the slicing of a pie
and each slice becomes
the name of a poem,
like a table of contents.
I wake, think this thing over, then drop off
only to see the pie again.
How clever I think I am
to have thought up such a grand idea,
worried though, there won't be enough pie
to go around.
In the morning, I can't imagine
what any of it means, it seemed so important
and yet, I don't remember
what kind of pie it was,
or know for sure if I ever knew.

During the morning I pass the stack of books
on the floor, one piled on top of the other.
These are the books I want to read
as soon as possible.
The stack is six foot three.
Later, I buy two more books
and a step-stool
so I won't fall adding the new books to the stack.
Soon I'll have to move to a new house,
one with higher ceilings it seems.

Night brings a meteor shower,
stars falling on the average of
37 miles a minute, and me
taking a blanket out in the yard
at midnight, laying myself down,
and waiting for something to move.

Looking Back

Last night I thought of Orpheus
as I looked back over my shoulder,
the poet and musician of old
who moved rocks and trees to dance.
He possessed magical powers
and a magical gift for life
and all these hundreds of years later
I wish I had something of his gift.
I could perhaps match his tragedy --
lack of faith in himself and love.
He looked back over his shoulder
and lost Eurydice forever.
I spent yesterday evening with Andrew.
We kissed goodnight and
after I settled in behind the steering wheel
and started the engine,
I dared to look over my shoulder
and nearly expected to find him
a pillar of salt
or a statue of stone
or simply vanished into thin air
like a wisp of smoke
from one of his cigarettes.
I looked back.
I looked back and saw him skipping --
only two or three steps --
but he was skipping across the street.
And I knew that it was me
who lifted those heavy boots
and made them dance.

Leland's Departure

Another day.
Leland's gone.
Dad comes, pack him up, gone.
To Oklahoma cold pan far from dead mama.
Bathtub blood and cat see no see don't know.
Sycamores eyes funny gone.
Empty new gone.
Why good.
Why no.
Why gone.
Why not me.
Stabbing gone.
Wrestle up laugh so fast no lunch so fast gone.
New and gone and us stuck jail bad scars kill mom
dead mom kill knife gone heaven Leland gone.
Oklahoma dad knife today and court and judge
no dad me stuck dog
seven one no mom new bed eyes talk
coming gone coming gone
gone for good cat dead far fast judge dad kill
jail mom gone knife why missing stuck me good-bye.
Leland leave Leland gone Leland
dad stab mom in bathtub.
Different dad, one in jail, one in Oklahoma.
I'm stuck here. I've been here longer.
I want to go home too.

_____ **SUSAN ESTABROOK**

Lake of Redemption

I'm always surprised, as I sit in the food park,
how many people I don't know.
So many feet in strange shoes, so many
muffins between strange eyes, so many
babies born after mine,
when I could swear he's only been here a minute.
Fry, flash, combination gringo
a necklace of blue dots
swirling light-wise to hover,
electric and real, under the last-named
Heir to a forest being cut down and
  shaved into postage stamps.
That woman over there is too young to be a mother,
but her child doesn't know that
as he drinks his fill.
Children see only the eyes and breast and the
  smile of their mother.
They learn to hear hands as a slap.
They learn to see words as a wall
  too high to scale.

I think of coffee as my lake of redemption.
It sizzles down-size atom by atom
and drains earthward to a
brown sea
tangled with confused nets
and silver bodies flip-flopping for a chance,
just a chance
to come up for air
one last time.

Lace

I lace him into my poems,
string him into the long, wide berth
of everyday petals.
A hint transcended
enveloping dreamtime cactus and other succulents.
I narrow my eyes to glimpse the horizon.
I see not gold but a lighter fabric,
stretched to snapping.
It bounces the moon to a closer orbit, where
it pulls at my skin like a tide
    of quantum plasma.
I could never replace the cells they took
without asking. They left me
raw and open,
but I've sutured myself closed.
I don't know where my moods come from,
or why I can't feel comfortable, even
in my favorite chair.
It suits me, sitting forward, turning from
the strong eyes that don't forgive.
Black roses prick my hands as I
try to brush away their shadow.
A once-bitten apple, rabbits in
elliptical bottles   truncation
    leave
He can't sleep with his head on my shoulder,
he told me.
My heart keeps him awake.
I can see it pounding right now, making
Mickey Mouse look like he's got hiccups.
What pours forth is red,
draws fingers of fire
and weaves itself into
my own white lace.

A Dark So Deep

He should have willed his knuckle bones to me.
I would have strung them together
into a necklace to wear around my neck
so that I'd always have a part of him
touching me.

When the dark grew too wide,
he put one foot in front of the other
and walked into water
and kept walking
until the water pressed with such force
against his temples, he no longer
remembered his feet.

He should have thought
how he wasn't just going away.
He should have thought
how he was leaving me.
If he didn't want those fingers
that he drew along my collar bone,
that he stuck into my cunt
like he was looking for honey --
if he didn't want those fingers
he should have known
I did. His life
wasn't just his own.
It was mine, his fingers
were mine, his arms
his cock, his face
his tongue was mine
and that dark, too, the dark that
pushed down so hard
he had to run from it,
that was mine.

I knew that dark
just like he did.
I suckled it until it
bled me dry. It banged me
against the dresser bureau and
tore my dress, it held me by the throat,
it slit my crotch,
it stole my babies,
it sawed off my breasts,
it slashed my face,
it called me whore and stupid and blind,
and every time
I crawled and stumbled up and groped
and found his hand.

How could there be a dark so deep
he could reach out with those fingers
those fingers
those fingers
and not find mine?

Erected Recollections

Remembering circus trains lurching through
Pasadena, Monrovia, Azusa, and Cucamonga.
Popjack, crackergum, peacorn -- a dyslexic carny's moan.
Sweet carmeled popcorn candy and prizes
    at munchkin baby fingers.

The appreciative congregation from pediatric to geriatric
observes the magnificent three ring show
    of exquisite performers.
Cracking whips tame ferocious cats with
fanged claws extended leap through fired hoops.
Dangling ribbons fly off the Spanish red-haired voyager
standing on the back of the prancing white Arabian horse
featured in center ring.
Eight trapezes undulate with
accomplished masters somersaulting to lofty tent peaks.

In the glittering lights on the fairway
con men invite the naive to ponder the
shell games, tattooed lady, fatman, midget quintuplets,
Siamese twins, two-headed cow
and all for one thin dime.

Hashslinger

in but without definition, waiting
now will with toil, knotting never
1991 jutted from lest the face brighten
seldom of minister to the grape
share the position within, without
leave from the volumes dotting
never giving the rear view, whether distant
saving solace send more
giving having form content east west
must build rebuild layer . . . no
undo now, now they undo
sense or, nonsense fosters time
selling sharing all the dreams
far to ten and one-half
pen failure will put up the pines
red yellow blue black
several few and none singing
summoning for the smile
relief in the absence
colliding idioms
not covered stirring.

Aime Lindsay - My dad used to bribe me -- a quarter a poem. I memorized *Jabberwocky* and I was hooked! Now I use poetry -- the reading, writing and community of it -- to remember and reconnect all the details. I write when I feel most alone; when my heart hurts or sings and I can't get it out any other way.

Alexandra Maeck - Poetry is a way there.

Anderson Stone - Music and poetry have been the two passions of my life. The choice was poet or musician. I can't carry a tune.

Charles Bischoff - Since poetry is words and is not words, writing poetry helps me in lessening the chasm between myself and my language.

Corey Slavin - To me poetry is a current that connects my physical being with my spirituality.

Danelia Wild - I write to claim my life, to claim the spaces between the breaths where I hide.

David Widup - I write because I don't know any other way.

Deanne Ivlev - Poetry is in my blood, as is blood in my poetry -- it simply is who I am from seed.

diana jean - Poetry is how I describe the world, me, in particular, with splashes of color that break up the shades of gray.

Ed Harrington - Hands down, poetry is the most exciting thing you can do, including sex. The afterglow from making a poem lasts longer than that of making love. In sex the withdrawal can be too quick, people pull away. The poem doesn't do this. It tapers off like a candle burning itself out, like a candle should.

Eileen Adele Hale - Poetry is the knife, and the water, and the light at the end of the tunnel. And the tunnel.

Estrellita Mendez - The poem is a frail lover sent out to walk the streets. Sometimes the streets are covered in glass. The poem gets bloody, leaves a messy trail. But always at the end the poem arrives at a place where there's something waiting, something that shivers. I make poems to be led to that shivering.

Fran Fisher - I write to be free -- free to look inside myself and let my feelings flow out. It's the poetry of my soul.

Genez Waite - I write because it's a chance to be honest and to explore myself. Poetry gives me the opportunity to be part of a community sharing in a tradition of writing and reading.

Jo Scott - Writing hurts -- but my compulsion to be understood overrides that. Poetry leaves me both frightened and purged.

Jack Grapes - Poetry begins at the beginning, and takes you all the way to the end. It's so life giving, and life affirming, and so bloody beautiful, no wonder few of us can stand to look it straight in the eye, opening our arms all the while to the terrible and lovely things it has to offer.

Joyce Stein - Poetry forces me to examine myself so other people can understand how much alike we are.

Lori Grapes - My son is two and I've found color: oranges and lemons. Purple Play-Doh. Scarlet Jello. It leaves one speechless, the way trees and lakes do. Poetry is another continent altogether, but the sensation of writing it is like that of discovering new worlds through my son's eyes.

Maxine Landis - Poetry is life. Life is poetry. Poetry helps you think, stimulates the creative juices that keep you going.

Michael Andrews - To be a poet takes an irrational commitment to communication that is a compulsion beyond the control of an artist. I have several compulsions: knowledge is one, making is another, and I suppose communicating is a third. When I say compulsion, I mean I have no rational excuse. No one would rationally choose to be a poet considering the abuse one takes to do it.

Mifanwy Kaiser - Poetry is the breath of life.

Mimi Nelson-Takiguchi - Poetry born of truth is like air and water. It flows with time like the tide.

Patricia L. Scruggs - A poem is a lot like a telegram. So much said in a short space, so much the reader has to fill in from her own experience. Sometimes when I read a poem I think that poet stole my life.

Stellasue Lee - I write because I have to. It's been challenging to make sense out of the first 50 years. I'm learning to have fun with the language, not to take myself so seriously. Most importantly I've learned that the things that are real are the things unseen and that the things that are seen are temporal, in flux.

Stephanie Hager - It's what makes my heart beat faster . . . makes my heart beat . . . makes my heart.

Susan Estabrook - I don't like writing, I like having written.

Terri Niccum - I write poetry because if and when I finally get it right it's my chance to level with myself. I think we tell ourselves a lot of lies just to get through life but poetry only resonates if there's truth to it. The funny thing is that when I finally succeed in telling myself what's what, it's like someone else far wiser, someone out there is saying it. So I write to uncover and acknowledge that older and deeper part of myself.

Warren Hill - Poetry brings the opportunity to see things differently, a shift in perception, which I experience as a true miracle of acceptance.